EVEN WHEN I CRY

Even When I Cry

Ruth Vaughn

moody press
chicago

© 1975 by
THE MOODY BIBLE INSTITUTE
OF CHICAGO

Library of Congress Cataloging in Publication Data
Vaughn, Ruth.
    Even when I cry.

    1. Meditations. I. Title.
BV4832.2.V38   242   75-14258
ISBN 0-8024-2389-2

Second Printing, 1976

Printed in the United States of America

FOR
Bill,
whose human love has
welcomed me
at whatever hour
I've come

Even when I cry

God welcomes,
          pardons,
                    cleanses,
                              strengthens,
                                        renews,
                                                  empowers,
                                                            loves.

Prologue

Rejection,
Words of condemnation,
Tears,
Darkness,
Failure.

How difficult it was to believe in God's love! I had nothing to offer Him. Surely He, too, would cast me out of His presence.

But when
  Through my tears
    I dared to look,
I found Him standing with me,
    Loving me,
    Welcoming me—
  Even when I cry.

"Is it true?" I whispered.

"May I really be in Your presence and stay, enjoy, accept Your love, Your strength, Your welcome?"

"Anytime," He said.

"You mean I can come to You
  Even when I've not been wise?
  Even when I've not been moral?
  Even when I've no gift to bring?"

His smile was deep. "Even then."

For the first time in my life, I had a glimpse of the meaning of divine love. God had the capacity for loving *all* of me *all* of the time! I was still for a long moment. How amazing! The love of God reached to me every moment of my life. Could it be true? I must be sure.

"You mean You will accept me
                Even when I cry?
In my hour of defeat
        As much as
                In my hour of triumph,
You will accept me?"
                "At whatever hour you come," He said.
                His face blurred through my grateful tears.
                "Thank You," I whispered.
                And I heard Him say, "You're welcome!"

In the Hour of Guilt

"Do you know what it's like to despise yourself?" wrote a young collegian in a note to me. "It's a black, fevered cloud that threatens suffocation. The yellow streaks of light that slit the cloud appear like tawny tigers that stare through amber eyes, just waiting to pounce upon your gasping, raspy breaths."

In the hour of self-hatred, we can, if we will look, find God standing with us. His steady eyes look into ours with no revulsion, no shock, no scorn for our sins. There is only love. And with sudden insight, we know the amazing truth that He accepts us *just as we are* in that hour. He does not expect us to break any habits, change any patterns of thought, remedy our despicableness before we come to Him. He only asks that we come, that we give our life's controls to Him. *He* will break the habits, change the thought patterns, remedy the despicableness.

The young collegian who wrote the above note to me carried a heavy weight of guilt, and he felt he must change his life before he could come to God. He wrote in greater detail of his problem:

"I know about God. Do I ever!

"I can quote all sixty-six books of the Bible in order. I can quote the fifth, sixth, and seventh chapters of Matthew letter-perfect. I have attended Sunday school every Sunday of my life, prayer meeting every Wednesday, and four high school youth camps!

11

"But after I came to college, I joined a motorcycle club. Soon I was introduced to the world of drugs. I thought this held the answers for my life. I kept trying heavier and heavier stuff, and at times I felt I had found *reality*. I could simply lie back and revel in *peace*.

"But it always came to an end. And back in the world again, I began to understand that this was not the way. My grades dropped; my parents were frantic. I was totally miserable in my guilt and self-hatred.

"One night I got down the Bible. Although I was familiar with the Book, it had somehow bored me. I had memorized much of it obediently. Mentally I had hung up long ago.

"I turned to Philippians 4:7 and read about the peace of God. Peace was what I had sought in my drug trips—and had found it, in a way, for moments at a time. But it was never lasting; it was never real.

"Despondency crushed in, and I decided to take another trip. Man, it was a bummer! I didn't know where I was, who I was, *if* I was. I really freaked out.

"But I ended up straight and realized all over again that drugs were not the answer. But what? Where?

"One night I was in the student union for a coke. I joined a group at a table. A rosy-cheeked freshman girl was talking earnestly about God. I listened and observed. It hit me: she really *believed*. She hadn't just memorized words from the Bible as I had done. She had based her life on them!

"When the group at the table broke up, I walked to the campus mall and stood looking at the sculptured Lamp of Learning. I remembered a verse where God said, 'Come unto me . . . and I will give you rest' (Matthew 11:28).

"I ran my fingers through my hair. *I've known those words as long as I can remember. But I've never really believed them. Can it be that I can simply come? Just as I am?* I had nothing of value to offer: a transcript smeared with failing

grades, a life messed up with drugs and futility, a burden of
guilt and self-hatred that threatened to crush me.

" 'Come,' He said.

"I took a deep breath and dared. 'God,' I whispered, 'I
come to You now if You'll have me. I've mouthed a lot of
words about You and love and peace all my life. But they
were just that—mere mouthings— The tears started in my
eyes as I felt Him near. 'Until now, God, until now!' "

This young collegian found welcome in God's presence in
his hour of guilt. He found welcome *just as he was.* The important thing was not what he brought to God. The important thing was what God made of what he brought. In a
moment of time, God pardoned, cleansed, forgave, redeemed.

Only today I received a letter from him. I had written to
ask permission to use his story in this chapter. His reply included some of the wisdom he had learned about the hour
of guilt.

"In that moment as I stood on the mall, I had to face my
total unworthiness of God's love. I suppose, for the first time
in my life, I had the acute realization that I had nothing to
offer. Until I got mixed up with drugs, I could offer my Bible
knowledge, my church attendance, my self-righteousness. But
that night I came to understand that becoming a Christian has
nothing whatever to do with self-righteousness. Becoming a
Christian has to do with *God!* And with Him there are no
stipulations other than one's own personal recognition of
need."

As I read the letter of this young man, now enrolled in his
first year of law school, my heart is thrilled at the manifesta-
tion of divine love in his life. Shorn of all sense of personal
goodness, he *came* to God in his hour of guilt and found
welcome, pardon, redemption.

When one is safely enfolded in the love of God, he can
learn to love himself rightly. He will find the longing to

live creatively. He will yearn to be all that God would have him to be in this life and the next. He will dare to dream with God the highest dream. He will accept the challenge to become a bigger person than he thought possible.

What life-changing, life-challenging, life-fulfilling powers flood our lives when we *come just as we are* and find welcome. God's love is amazing. We can find His acceptance, even in the hour of guilt.

> *For when we were yet without strength, in due time Christ died for the ungodly.*
> *For scarcely for a righteous man will one die: yet peradventure for a good man some would even dare to die.*
> *But God commendeth his love toward us, in that, while we were yet sinners, Christ died for us.*
>
> ROMANS 5:6-8

In the Hour of Commitment

"I didn't want to be treated as a girl-like-all-others but as Anne-on-her-own merits," wrote the young Jewish girl Anne Frank in her diary.

One of the first things I learned as a child was that God considers each of His children as special, different from all others. The plan He charts for each child is distinctly unique; none is a Xerox copy of another's. I understood and gloried in that fact until it crashed into my consciousness that neither would His plan be a Xerox copy of mine!

The plan *God* charted for my life was not the one which *I,* "as a girl-like-all-others," planned. It was one designed specifically for "Ruth-on-her-own merits." And his vision of that girl was bigger than mine!

I dreamed of love and marriage. When I was a freshman in college I, "as-a-girl-like-all-others," made my plans for fulfillment with a young, handsome boy who had asked me to marry him. But when I finally got around to praying seriously about the matter, God said no!

He had a plan different from mine!

I was appalled.

I ran to my room on the second floor of a college dormitory and argued, fought, and cried. I was certain that if I followed His plan, it would lead me straight to spinsterhood. I explained; I rationalized; I exhorted.

Finally I shut up—and listened.

15

He asked me to give to Him the plan I had so carefully worked out in detail. He asked me to void the plan completely and commit all of my future to Him.

My father used to say, "God can choose a plan for your life that will please *you* better than any plan you can choose for yourself." Men in the Bible may have proven it true. My parents may have proven it true. But in regard to my own young life, I thought it was a gamble.

Here I had a plan worked out which involved a handsome, nice, Christian young man. Surely I could find happiness with him. To tear up the plan with none other in the offing was a gamble.

"God can choose a plan for your life that will please *you* better than any plan you can choose for yourself. Notice," my father would continue, "I didn't say that He has a plan that would please *Him* better. That is true; it would. But I said He had a plan that would please *you* better than any plan you can work out for yourself."

That was only a promise. Would I gamble on God's knowledge, God's love, God's wisdom? Could it be that He really could choose better for *me* than I could?

Coud I trust Him that much?

I took a deep breath and made my life's choice. I would tell the nice young man that I could not share his life. I would give myself wholly to the lordship of God, walking wherever He led.

There is no way that I know to explain the events and emotions of that moment other than to say it was a meeting of two hearts—mine and God's. And in that moment of total honesty, I turned the controls of my life over to Him. And I began attempting to look at life from His viewpoint.

I changed my life plans.

And for awhile I walked alone.

And then one day in a college speech class I saw a young man who was constructed in just the way I would construct young men if that were my business. With typical feminine instinct, I began to plan strategy that would result in his inviting me to an important, upcoming banquet.

After class that day, I went to the post office. On the way back to the dormitory, I saw a delphinium blue dress in a store window. I paused, enraptured. It was the most beautiful dress I had ever seen! Surely if I could wear that dress to the Friday night party, he would not only ask me for a date to the banquet—*he* would *plead!*

Then I looked at the price tag.

"Oh, wow!" Practicing purple prose, I hurriedly went to my room and placed a call to my father. I tried every feminine wile I knew to convince my father that I *needed* the delphinium blue dress. I begged. I teased. I wept. But my father was immovable. I did *not* need a dress that expensive for a party!

I finally accepted defeat and hung up. But my father's refusal did not deter me. I was bound and determined to wear that delphinium blue dress to the party because I *knew* it would dazzle *him* into my companionship for the banquet!

The days passed. I tried several projects to make some money; but they all backfired.

Finally, on Thursday before the party, I went to the post office and found a letter from my father. In it was the money for the dress.

I screamed with delight and skipped all the way to chapel.

That chapel service was my undoing.

A missionary spoke that morning, and my heart surged on an upbeat at the challenge of her work. When she had finished, the president of the college took an offering to help buy equipment for her return to the field.

I was in tears. The challenge was so great. She was doing such a marvelous work. She must go back. She must have equipment.

I sincerely wished I could help, but I knew I could not. The small salary I earned at the college went to my tuition. I had no money of my own.

You could give your blue dress, He said.

Oh, no! I drew back in my seat. *Oh, no! That dress is important to me!*

That equipment is important in My work.

But this money is just for me! I protested. *My father wanted to make me happy.* And oh, *that dress would make me happier than anything!*

Anything? I thought we had agreed that you would try to look at things from My viewpoint. If so, which is the most important?

The offering plate came then. I looked at it for a long moment. I clearly remembered the hour of commitment. Perhaps I would *still* walk alone.

I took a deep breath and opened my father's letter. I drew the bills from it and slipped them into the plate.

As the plate passed on, my heart knew a sense of deep peace. It was a meeting of hearts again—God's and mine!

I went to the party on Friday night in my old, red wool. If *he* was to take special notice of me, it would have to be God's doing.

He asked me to go with him to the banquet.

Later, he asked me to marry him.

And I did!

Now, after almost twenty years of marriage, I can see how far superior God's plan was to the one I had worked out for myself. God's plan included a boy who personified my dreams come true. He was not as a "boy-like-all-the-others." He was a boy who was stronger than I; a boy whose feet were firmly grounded in reality while I soared aloft with impossible dreams and grand ideals; a boy who gladly, bouyantly walked with me and God on the highest roads of life; a boy designed for "Ruth-on-her-own merits."

What beautiful life plans are awaiting us when we meet God in the hour of commitment! He will guide, direct, companion, strengthen through all of the rest of life, even in the hour of commitment.

> *Delight thyself also in the Lord; and he shall give thee the desires of thine heart.*
> *Commit thy way unto the Lord; trust also in him; and he shall bring it to pass.*
>
> PSALM 37:4-5

In the Hour of Fear

Robert Frost wrote that there are two fears which we should have—fear of God, lest we prove unworthy of this One who knows us best; and fear of man, lest he misunderstand us and withdraw his fellowship from us. These are valid, wholesome fears. But there is an unhealthy fear that besets most of us: fear of the future. So much of our time and energy is spent in worry about what *could* happen. Our lack of knowledge and security about what the future holds assume hideous forms and gigantic dimensions which rob our nights of sleep, our days of serenity.

I understand the hour of fear, because I have lived in its icy atmosphere. I remember a night I could not sleep and arose to wander about the house. Finally, I went into the den, grabbed my notebook, and began to write:

> I have grown afraid of life. I have taken my life back into my own hands, because I am afraid of what God will do to me. He has allowed this problem to enter my life, and I now live in fear. But it (the fear) lives and grows only as long as I try to overcome it myself. It is cast out only when I deliberately remember Jesus. Not that He has promised to cast out the *reason* for the fear—but He has promised by His presence to cast out the *fear*.

I paused and reread my words. *How easy it is to articulate theory,* I thought. *How difficult to put it into practice.* And then I remembered Shelly. Of all the people who have triumphed in the hour of fear, Shelly ranks near the top. I let my notebook drop from my hands as I remembered the story she had told me.

"Terminal cancer," the doctor said, and the words seemed to bounce around the room, and hit the mahogany window-sill, to beat against the windowpane like a frantic moth.

"No!" she whispered. "No!"

"I'm sorry," the doctor said. His face sagged, and his eyes were weary. "I'll want you to see a specialist, of course."

She nodded absently. "Yes. Yes. Anything you say."

Outside his office, her mind whirled with broken fragments of thoughts and emotions. The passersby on the street and the pale spring sunlight all seemed unreal. Frantically she tried to find some means of bringing her world back into focus.

It simply was not fair! She had been cheated. She was only twenty-three. She had not accomplished the things she had set out to do. Because of her family's poverty, she was still working her way through college. She would not finish for another year. There had been a few dates, a few wild promises. But she had not had time to know love. She wanted to marry, have babies, grow old. Rebellion welled up in her at such injustice.

Her anger braced her as if it were a stimulant. Her chin grew firm again. Her step hastened her to her favorite coffee shop, where she seated herself at the window overlooking the ocean. This was her favorite spot. Here she could think.

"Terminal cancer," the man had said.

She was going to die. In a matter of months from this second in which she was breathing and whole, she would be—dead.

She could not remember when the fear of death had begun. It was probably at the funeral of some forgotten relative, when the alien coffin, the strong perfume of flowers, the scraps of whispered adult conversation had erected nameless horrors in her while she had been too young to understand. Perhaps, too early, she had read a book stimulating fear of the unknown. Whatever its inception, the terror had lain inside her for many years. She did not want to die. She was afraid.

The waitress brought the coffee.

As she stirred the dark liquid, she let her thoughts go. *This cannot be real. When one faces death, it should be wild and noisy. There should be the crashing of great cymbals and the turmoil of trumpets and harps. But here I sit quietly in my familiar coffee shop, and there are only the sounds of the rise and fall of voices, the hum of traffic outside. It can't be true!*

But she knew that it was. She had not let its truth find its way to that soft part of her where it could slash and destroy. She was holding it in abeyance, looking at her calamity carefully, critically. But she knew its truth.

Let not your heart be troubled (John 14:1).

The words pushed from the backroads of her mind. She frowned. She wanted no part of Scripture now. Her mother had made her memorize chapters of it in her childhood. But it held no help for her now.

Let not your heart be troubled.

If her mother had been here, she could have used this phrase to point out clearly the irrelevance of the ancient Bible to twentieth century problems. But here she sat with a death sentence, and the only Scripture she remembered was "Let not your heart be troubled." Typically unrealistic!

But as she sat there, other words were struggling through the thick darkness of her mind toward consciousness.

In my Father's house are many mansions: If it were not so, I would have told you. I go to prepare a place for you. And if I go and prepare a place for you, I will come again, and receive you unto myself; that where I am, there ye may be also.... I am the way, the truth, and the life: no man cometh unto the Father, but by me (John 14:2-3, 6).

With a quick gesture of impatience, she pushed the coffee cup from her and rose. Grabbing her purse, she strode to the cash register.

The small, dark man at the counter greeted her with characteristic enthusiasm. Even in her despair, she could not keep from responding a little. His inner joy released itself in irresistible smiles that he turned upon his customers and the passersby.

"Today you are beautiful as usual," he rejoiced. "Your skin is like good dairy cream. Your being here today has made my day brighter because you always bring sunshine."

Absurdly, tears sprang to her eyes. For a moment, she struggled for self-control. But everything had started to topple.

"Geno," she whispered, "I have cancer. I am going to die."

Quietly he led her back to the table where she had been sitting. He shoved a large, scratchy, man's handkerchief into her hands. He sat with her in silence until the tears had finally ceased.

"Geno," she whispered, "what am I going to do?"

"Do you believe in the resurrection?" he asked gravely.

She stared at him. "You mean Christ's resurrection? How does that possibly fit in here?"

"It fits because if you believe He walked out of that borrowed tomb that first Easter morning, you don't have to cry."

"Oh, Geno," Shelly said bitterly, "You aren't going to give me, 'Let not your heart be troubled,' are you?"

"What else is there at a moment like this?"

"Well, surely something more realistic, more relevant."

"If so, mankind has not found it. If you believe Christ is alive today, you know that His Word is true. If you believe His Word is true, you know that death is not a dead-end street. It is only a door into a larger life."

"Do you believe that?"

"With all my heart."

"But it's easy for you! Platitudes come easily to the unscathed. No doctor has hurled a death sentence into your lap today!"

"No. You are right. Not today. Four months ago."

The color drained from her cheeks. Her eyes were filled with horror.

"Geno—I'm sorry—I didn't know—I—"

"It's all right. Don't look so distressed. I'm not, because I *know* Him, who arose bodily and who now lives at the right hand of the Father *and* in my heart."

"How long do you have?"

"Maybe two years, maybe three."

"You make me feel so ashamed."

"Don't. I felt just like you when I first walked out of my doctor's office. I went straight to my church and knelt at the altar. And He came *within,* bringing such light *upon* and *within* me that the darkness evaporated and has never come again. My heart need not be troubled. I believe He went to prepare a place for me and that He will come and receive me unto Himself. Is that something to fear? No, how can one fear love?"

For some time, they sat in silence, thinking and watching the shadows lengthen and the sun drop toward the misty ocean. Then a waiter came and asked Geno about a kitchen problem, and the moment was shattered.

Shelly walked slowly on the sidewalk. She passed a Roman Catholic church. Since she was a lifelong Protestant, her steps did not slow until she stood across from the statue in the garden. It was one she had seen often and never cared for, but she had respected it as a symbol. It was Jesus Christ standing with His heart exposed, His hands lovingly inviting the sinner to come to Him.

Impulsively she went to the statue and stood before it. What had Geno said? "How can one fear love?"

And *He* had said one long-ago day, "Let not your heart be troubled; ye believe in God, believe also in me. In my house are many mansions. I go to prepare a place for you."

Her voice was trembling with tears as she whispered, "Help me not to be afraid. Help me to know Your love so fully, so keenly, that I cannot fear."

I sat in the den and thought of Shelly's indomitable spirit. Still pursuing her studies, she had recently written to me of her straight-*A* report card, a book she had read, a concert she had attended. Only at the bottom of the letter did she speak of the incurable disease, and then it was with triumph: "I have found that when I have faith, fear is driven out of my heart. When fear is dead, life begins. Here. And over there. Ruth, I do not fear the transition from life here to life with Christ. As Geno said: 'How can one fear love?' "

Tears fell on my notebook as I lifted it to read the sentences I had written, "But it (the fear) lives and grows only when I try to overcome it myself. It is cast out only when I deliberately remember Jesus. Not that He has promised to cast out the *reason* for the fear but that He has promised, by His very presence, to cast out the *fear.*"

Shelly had overcome fear. I *could* overcome fear if I would practice the truth I knew in my heart. In my hour of fear, I could deliberately remember Jesus, move into His presence, and find that *He* could cast out the *fear.* As Geno had said: "How can one fear love?"

I may replace fear with love because Jesus said He would accept me, even in the hour of fear.

> *There is no fear in love; but perfect love casteth out fear: because fear hath torment. He that feareth is not made perfect in love.*
>
> *We love him, because he first loved us.*
>
> 1 John 4:18-19

In the Hour of Frustration

Peace is not something we can wrap in a package or store on a shelf. In fact, peace is not a "something." It is a personality: Jesus Christ Himself. We can focus on His peace and *be* at peace. We can focus on the anxieties and pressures of our lives and be filled with frustration, or we can consciously walk with Him and maintain our poise. If we allow life's problems to control our conscious thought until we are oblivious of Him, our poise will be shattered. The *choice* is ours.

My mother wrote to me one time that there are two things about life to consider: what happens and how we react to what happens. She said that the second was of far greater importance than the first. We cannot control what happens in our lives; we can control how we react to what happens.

When I was nineteen years old, I married a young minister, and he took me to his first parish. Although I had grown up in a parsonage, I was ill prepared. The role of a minister's daughter is drastically different from the role of minister's wife. The role of a carefree collegian, from which I had just emerged, was several light years away from the role of the responsible minister's wife. From a life where my studies ranged from "fundamentals of art" to "theories of acting," I stepped into a life where my course of study ranged from "housing a complete Sunday school in a three-room apartment (mine)" to "survival on a salary of twenty-five dollars per week."

27

And I learned—as best I could.

I learned to be missionary president, vacation Bible school supervisor, church pianist, Sunday school teacher, hostess to the district superintendent, athletic director, hospital visitor, and comforter in the face of death.

I learned to make curtains out of sheets, doilies from scraps, little shirts from big ones, one thousand different meals from hamburger, and stew from nothing whatever.

And I gave up the luxury of growing up an inch at a time. When I walked into that small church with the three-room parsonage in the back, I had to grow up all the way in the space of a heartbeat. And there were times I wistfully yearned for youth.

One Monday afternoon the frustration that had been building within me reached its limit. The junior class had stopped up the plumbing on Sunday morning. Torrents of rain had poured through the hole in the bedroom ceiling. A kindergartner had spilled ink on my new tablecloth. Another had printed his name on the stove.

I scrubbed vigorously on a pan. No time to think of that book about which my college chum had written me. No time to think of the new dress my mother-in-law had sent me. No time to think of my nineteen-year-old cousin being crowned that night as college queen. No time to think! There were too many things to *do!*

There was a Sunday school lesson to study, teen activities to plan, a missionary meeting to prepare, visiting to do—all between relentless sprints to an ever ringing telephone. And I was only nineteen!

At that moment I looked about. The fingerprints from the children's classes all over the house loomed clearly. The worn place on the couch seemed suddenly dreadful. The clothes would not dry. The rain flooded out the sun. The Jello would not jell. The icebox would not defrost. The ink stain on the tablecloth would not budge. And the stew had stuck in the bottom of the pan and clung with stubborn persistence!

The water in the potatoes boiled over on the stove while the telephone rang on and on and on. And above it all came the demanding thoughts, *I must do this! I must do that!* Incessantly they came!

Suddenly I stopped scrubbing the pan and set it on the cabinet with finality, muttering, " 'This is the way; walk ye in it.' You said that, Lord! And here I am!" My voice broke in a sob, for in that moment, my mind clutched the fear that had darted into it so many times. And with its coming, the building frustration reached the breaking point.

Lord, I've found that this job is bigger than I am! Next time I'll try raising ducks, Lord! Home missions is too much for me!

And the flood of my dammed-up tears broke forth. I ran into the small bedroom and hurled myself onto the bed as the storm of frustration and feelings of inadequacy overwhelmed me, and I felt I would surely be overcome in the roar of the tide.

"Lord," I whispered, "Are you here? Can you help me?"

A knock at the door dammed up the tears again. I smoothed the ravages on my face and politely answered. It was a red-haired, freckle-nosed boy who had come into our church through our vacation Bible school in the summer.

He sat on the couch, covering the worn spot exactly. He looked timidly at me and said, "Mrs. Vaughn, I wrote an essay last night on 'The Most Important Things in My Life.' I thought maybe you would like to see it."

I took the piece of paper and began to read the boyish scrawl. It went like this:

"This essay is different than the one I would have written last year! It is different because I have a new friend. I made lots of new friends this summer—but one is the most important of them all. So I will say that the most important thing in my life is God! My pastor taught me that.

"Next I would say that the second most important thing to me is love! My Friend gives to me divine love, and He helps me to love others instead of trying to fight them like I used to do!"

I looked up through misted eyes and again surveyed my parsonage.

In that moment, the ink stain and the fingerprints retreated. The crayoned names would wash off the stove. The sun would shine again. The clothes would dry. The hole in the roof could be repaired.

The worn spot on the couch was indiscernible because of a blue-eyed boy who sat there with his eyes shining with a happy glow and youthful eagerness. He had found a new Friend, a new philosophy, all because we had been there at that time, at that place on the road of life. He did not know I was only nineteen. He did not know I was inexpert at directing vacation Bible schools and running a busy parsonage. He only knew I was important enough to share his essay.

I held the rumpled piece of paper to my heart. Through it God had assured me that He was with me in the hour of frustration. He would guide me, a youthful pioneer, through the demanding parsonage life until I could cope as calmly and matter-of-factly as my own mother. And I whispered, "Lord, keep the ducks! I'll carry on with Your plans for now!"

I looked at the little boy, and my heart flooded with gratitude for participating in his life. I whispered, "Thank You, Lord. Thank You from the depths of my heart."

The lesson that I learned that day was that frustration could ruin my life unless I *choose* to cultivate the habit of remembering who it is who walks with me. When I do that, in the hour of my frustration and inadequacies, I can rely on Him. The quietness that comes from the knowledge that He is there will, in time, restore my poise.

What amazing love! God walks with me—and will fill me with His peace, even in the hour of frustration.

> *Hast thou not known? hast thou not heard, that the ever-lasting God, the Lord, the Creator of the ends of the earth, fainteth not, neither is weary? there is no searching of his understanding.*
>
> *He giveth power to the faint; and to them that have no might he increaseth strength.*
>
> *Even the youths shall faint and be weary, and the young men shall utterly fall:*
>
> *But they that wait upon the Lord shall renew their strength; they shall mount up with wings as eagles; they shall run, and not be weary; and they shall walk, and not faint.*
>
> ISAIAH 40:28-31

In the Hour of Self-pity

We all have basic assumptions about how we should be treated in life. When these are not met, we often allow ourselves to sink into self-pity and resentment about life for treating us so cruelly. This is our *choice.* We are the product of what we *choose,* under the circumstances of our lives, to be. We are not just the product of what life does to us.

The hour of self-pity is a luxury. If we are really honest, we have to admit that we enjoy it. Someone told me of a friend who was upset because I had not yet been by to see her while I was speaking in that city. My informer grinned as she told me. "She's really hoping you won't come by at all!" Surprised, I asked why. "Because she's enjoying self-pity so much!"

Does that sound extreme? I doubt that it is. We luxuriate in self-pity, not realizing how destructive it can be. Not only does self-pity destroy valuable time and energy; it can also destroy our life's perspective. It can destroy our integrity.

Self-pity when our basic assumptions about life are not met is our *choice.* But there is an alternative. It is hard and not nearly so much fun as feeling sorry for ourselves, but by *an act of our will,* we can *choose* to bring our disappointments in life to God, and together we can work them out.

A young woman in one of my classes shared with me her experience in the hour of self-pity and the destructive effects incurred. She suggested that I share it with you.

*   *   *

My husband was called to preach the night after our son
was born. Instead of coming to see me in the hospital (a
basic assumption I held about the way a new mother should
be treated by her husband), he had chosen to go to church.
That stung me. But when he came to see me the next morning and told me he had answered the call to preach, I was
even more disturbed. When he brought me home from the
hospital and announced that he was going to quit his job so
he could go to college to prepare for the ministry, I became
intensely bitter. Almost all of my basic assumptions about
life revolved around the fact that women were to be keepers
of the home, mothers of the babies, and coddled treasures.
All of this was being violated.

I did not say a word. My mother had carefully trained me
that the man was the head of the house. The wife obeyed.
That was that.

I practiced the theory faithfully. But inside I was seething.

When the baby was three months old, we moved out of
our lovely house in our hometown and into a tiny apartment
in the town where Don's college was located. He had quit
his job as manager of a department in his company and had
gone to work in a grocery store from three to eleven. I suggested that I should get a job, but he insisted that I, too, must
go to school.

So the baby stayed at a baby-sitter's while I went to school
in the mornings. The baby and I stayed alone while Don
worked afternoons and evenings.

Life was made up of the taste of Spanish rice and macaroni
and cheese; the feel of hand-me-down clothing; the pungent,
acrid smell of the baby's diapers being plunged into the big,
gleaming tub at the laundromat; the challenge of big thick
books that I must conquer even though there was no will to
study.

Talk about self-pity! I was consumed with it. I cared nothing about Milton's writings, the study of Western civilization, or how to make a persuasive speech according to Monroe's Motivated Sequence. I wanted only to be a wife and mother in a nicely furnished house where I could prepare recipes with some meat other than hamburger. That was my *right* as a woman! I was not being treated fairly!

One morning I trudged across the campus to take a test. It was harder than I had expected. When I left the class, I was as low as I had ever been. I met Don, and we went to chapel. I did not sing because I did not feel like it. Don could force me to go to school when I did not want to go. He could even force me to live in a parsonage with him after school. But he certainly could not force me to sing in chapel! Mistreated I was, and I was going to lash back someway!

The minister who spoke in chapel that morning began with a presentation of the financial needs of the college. He asked that we bow our heads for prayer. Immediately I mouthed my usual petition, "God, please let us go back home where I can be treated like I should!"

Then the speaker asked everyone to stand who would try to give one hundred dollars in the next four weeks to help the college in its time of need. To my amazement, most of the student body responded—*including my husband!* I could not believe it! We were barely eking out an existence. I had no money for pretty furniture, nice clothes, interesting recipes. But he was going to give away one hundred dollars!

I do not know when I was ever so angry. It took all of my self-control to sit there during the rest of chapel.

When they finally got to the altar call, I walked out the door. To my surprise, Don followed me. I knew he had a class the next hour, and he never missed a class. *He never misses anything that has to do with the college,* I thought bitterly.

He walked with me in silence to the car. When he slid behind the wheel, I spoke for the first time.

"Don't you have a class?"

"Yes, but I'll take you home first."

"Thank you for your kindness," I said sarcastically.

He did not say anything.

I got into the car, and he drove me home. Almost before he stopped, I jumped out of the car. But instead of going back to the college, he turned off the ignition and followed me into the house.

I slammed my books on the table and whirled on him. "Why don't you go back to class? You know the only important thing in your life can't be ignored!"

He just looked at me.

My anger was mounting. "Why don't you leave?" I shouted.

"Because I don't want you to be mad."

I laughed. "You don't want me to be mad! You don't want me to be mad! Oh, how funny! Don't you know that I have been mad for a year?"

He looked surprised. "No, have you?"

"Have I? I had your baby. You should have rushed to see me. Where did you go? To church! You didn't care about me!

"I furnished your house carefully. I kept it clean. You were supposed to be contented and proud. What did you do? You sold it and told me I had to live in a parsonage!

"I had my family, my friends, my hobbies. You were supposed to enjoy them with me. What did you say? 'Give them all up. You are going to study Milton and Western civilization.'

"We had a good income. You were supposed to care for me and your children financially. But were you content to do that? Oh, no! You went to work in a grocery store to pay school bills."

As I stormed, I opened the closet door and pulled out my suitcase.

"When all of our friends back home are buying their first Buicks and bricking in a patio, we are driving an old VW and trying to pay tuition!"

He sat down heavily. "I didn't know you felt that way."

I began to sling clothes into the suitcase. "Of course, you didn't know. I have been all that a wife should be. You have been all that a husband should *not* be! But I have endured it without a word. I have lived in a shabby apartment, cooked hamburger, studied Monroe's Motivated Sequence, and never said a word. Not until now!"

I snapped the suitcase shut. "If you want to give one hundred dollars to your beloved college, you will give it on your own, because I will not be here. If you want a wife who can recite the merits of *Paradise Lost* to live in your parsonage, you will just have to find another."

With that I grabbed my suitcase and ran to the car. I put the key in the ignition and roared away.

Before I got to the freeway, I saw I needed gas. I pulled into a service station. While the attendant was filling the tank, I went into the green-tiled ladies' room to wash. The face in the mirror was a stranger's face, the eyes puffed, the lips pale, the hair brassy instead of blond under the fluorescent light. What had happened to the fresh-faced girl, so eagerly loving, of just one year ago?

After paying for the gas, I slowly pulled away.

"O God," I cried, "please be with me now."

I thought of what it would be like to be home again. Mother would love me. Daddy would putter around the room, muttering about Don. The beige and brown living

room—every chair, every picture selected for its beauty—
would be a haven. There I would have treatment and sur-
roundings in line with my basic assumptions about what
life should offer me. There, I knew, I would be wildly happy.

But would I?

"O God," I prayed desperately, "speak to me now."

But as I drove along, there was only the sound of the tires
whirling on the pavement, the sound of the clock ticking in
the silence.

About five o'clock I stopped for supper. The restaurant
was small, quiet, cozy. The woman in the next booth had a
baby. I watched her enviously. How happy she seemed, how
totally caught up in love! *Mothers are always caught up in
love,* I thought.

Aren't wives supposed to be, too?

I swallowed quickly. I almost looked around, although I
knew no one was standing there. But the words were so clear,
so compelling.

"Lord," I whispered, "was that You?"

But I knew the answer. Deep inside I knew the answer.

I sat in the restaurant and honestly faced the problem of
the past year. Don had violated my most basic assumptions
about life, and I had been consumed with self-pity. God was
spotlighting my hostilities. Dr. Shoemaker said:

> Perhaps there is no surer test for our real integrity than what
> we do with the insights which we discover in Christianity. If
> we head right into them, and let them reveal ourselves to us,
> we shall have integrity. If we reject or evade them, we shall
> have the dividedness of mind which is dishonest at the start,
> and becomes more neurotic as time goes on.

I knew the *choice* was mine. I could *choose* to continue
with my self-pity and let it destroy my marriage. Or I could
choose to bring my self-pity directly to God and, with Him,

work out new assumptions about life with which I could be happy and successful in my marriage. The choice was mine: *easy* self-pity which destroys or *hard* rearrangement of life values upon which to build.

"God, help me!" I cried. The tears fell through my fingers onto the table. I knew He was with me.

When I left the restaurant, I turned the car back toward the little apartment I had left.

It was late when I got home.

Quietly I pushed open the door and entered, careful to avoid the toys on the floor. The lamplight fell upon the soft beauty of the baby's face and upon the face of the man beside him.

They had fallen asleep on the couch, father and son, the man still fully dressed. The small boy was nestled in the curve of the man's arm, and the two faces, deep in sleep, were so alike that my heart stirred within me like a frozen brook beneath the snow.

I knelt beside them. I picked up the baby's chubby hand and kissed it. *Someday*, I thought, *some woman will have your happiness in the palm of her hand, my son. I hope she will be more generous than I have been to your father.*

Then I kissed Don's hand. " 'Whither thou goest, I will go,' " I whispered. " 'Thy people shall be my people, and thy God my God.' "

I kissed him again and quietly carried my suitcase into the bedroom to unpack. In my hour of self-pity, God had stood with me. My emotions were too strong to cope with alone. But He was there to help me correct my wrongdoing in the moment of decision and to continue to help me readjust my basic assumptions about the way life should treat me. It is too hard for me alone. But I can be adequate for the difficult when God controls.

*   *   *

His grace is sufficient. He will welcome, accept, pardon, and strengthen, even in the hour of self-pity.

> *I will say unto God my rock, Why hast thou forgotten me? why go I mourning because of the oppression of the enemy?*
>
> *As with a sword in my bones, mine enemies reproach me; while they say daily unto me, Where is thy God?*
>
> *Why art thou cast down, O my soul? and why art thou disquieted within me? hope thou in God: for I shall yet praise him, who is the health of my countenance, and my God.*

PSALM 42:9-11

In the Hour of Doubt

There are times in our lives when a kind of nightmare haunts us. We look upon our world and see no reflection of its Creator. God seems silent, absent, or dead.

Perhaps we should have in our churches a "Society of St. Thomas the Doubter," a place where people with honest doubts could seek as did that disciple who doubted the resurrection of Christ. "Except I shall see in his hands the print of the nails, and put my finger into the print of the nails, and thrust my hand into his side, I will not believe" (John 20: 25). Thomas wanted a kind of proof—but Thomas *cared!* He cared intensely that he find *truth*. He was still one of the twelve and one of the saints.

This may be a shocking concept to many people who feel that doubt is a sin. I have heard preachers say from the pulpit that they have never asked God why, nor have they ever had a moment of doubt about His existence. If that is true, I would believe their relationship with God to be rather strained or superficial. When one truly *cares* about truth, he experiences real doubt—doubt that seeks the truth. And when one doubts for the sake of knowing truth, when one disbelieves in God for the sake of a greater certainty of His existence, that one will be rewarded by deeper faith. Through doubt God is able to test, purge, and strengthen his saints. When one has the courage to doubt, then God may be found through a purer faith in that very moment when mere *assertions* about God have been cast away.

41

Perhaps the clearest example that I know of the hour of doubt is my father's experience. He began his pulpit ministry as a boy of fifteen years. Through the ensuing seventy years of his life, he faithfully preached the message he had learned as a child.

But when the love of his life, my mother, was swallowed in unconsciousness for thirteen months, that faith was shaken to its foundations. My father entered the torture house of faith where suffering demanded solemn scrutiny of beliefs: nothing was too sacred to question, nothing was off limits to doubt.

"If ye shall ask anything in my name, I will do it." (John 14:14). For seventy years, he had preached it as literal truth. In my mother's illness, he "asked" unceasingly. Nothing happened.

She simply lay in the deep beyond of the subconscious. He called to her, but there was no response. And he stood by her bed day after day watching for some sign of consciousness, but finding none. The only stirrings within her were moaning, groaning sounds, and the steady beat of a faithful heart.

Friends ceased to come to her room because they could not bear to see her as a "vegetable." Even the doctor said that he hoped for a massive heart attack to snuff out the breath of her being.

"If ye ask anything—"

The words haunted his mind, flitting in and out like a moth near a flame, teasing him with their familiarity, seemingly mocking a faith shaken to its foundations.

I, their youngest child, came and stood by his side. Together we lookd at the much-loved one lying inertly on the bed.

"God is love." That was her favorite portion of Scripture. The words were bitter. Love? She, of the smiling lips and sparkling eyes, who had rejoiced in spite of incurable illness,

had taught me, "God is love." If so, then what had happened
to all of His loving virtues: tenderness, protectiveness, affec-
tion, solicitude, answers to prayer? My father's agony was
deep.

St. Augustine understood this kind of suffering. He wrote:
"To thee, O Lord, I should have lifted up my mind for thee
to give it relief, but neither had I the will nor the power to
do so. And the difficulty was greater because, when I thought
of thee, nothing real and substantial presented itself to my
mind."

I sat by my mother's bed and watched my father in his war:
this tall strong man who had been the unmovable Rock of
Gibraltar to his children and parishoners through the years.
And now I realized, with sudden insight, that this had been
true because he had never developed a flair for piety. He had
always been courageously human—as he was now.

At age eighty-five, he did not walk about that small room
spouting pious thoughts from long habit. Instead he paced
the floor in purposeful battle. My heart rushed in pride for
him. He was not at all "like old soldiers in the dress uniform
of some forgotten war." Oh, no! His war was current, vio-
lent, *now*.

This man *cared* about truth. He *cared* about the sermons
he had preached from his pulpits. He *cared* about the precepts
he had carefully planted in the minds of his children. And
now, in that small room of unanswered prayer, he fought the
fires of his soul's agony to determine the truth of those precepts.

On the early February morning when my mother's body
died, my father lay asleep in the bed next to hers—the post he
had maintained through the long months of her illness. When
my brother awakened him, I took a deep breath. Daddy still
had few answers. He still struggled over "If ye ask anything—" He had asked; yet Mother was gone.

How would he react?

"What's wrong?" Daddy asked.

"Mother went to heaven a few minutes ago," Joe said gently.

The tears began slowly, softly down Daddy's cheeks. And then he said with a wistful smile, "She's happy."

And my heart surged on an upbeat of pride. He did not *understand* "Thus saith the Lord." But he *believed* it. He had prayed for understanding; he had found confusion. He had prayed for light; he had found darkness. But in the confusion, in the dark, he found a way to trust even though he could not see or understand.

A year later, my father had a massive heart attack. I stood by his side in the intensive care unit; and he said, "You know, I may not live."

"Daddy, you will. Of course, you will."

He shook his head wearily. "You know I may not live, and if I don't, you remember, God doeth all things well."

I kissed his hand. "I'll remember, Daddy."

But he was not satisfied. He moved his head to look at me keenly, summoning all of his strength in this moment. He knew that I loved him with a fierce deep love. He knew that I had watched him month after weary month in his war with God over Mother's illness. He knew I had listened many hours to his words of painful doubt. Now, as he poised between worlds, he had to make me understand he had found his peace. "Promise me," he whispered urgently, "promise me you'll always remember that God doeth all things well."

I kissed him and fervently promised.

I did not tell him that he need not have worried. I had understood all along. I had watched the battle; I had listened to the doubt—but I knew the soldier; I understood how much he *cared* about truth.

In looking at my father's hour of doubt, I find something of God's grace. His doubting clarified his thinking, toppled his false ideas, deepened his respect for truth. God was with him through it all, understanding and loving, leading him through the experiences of suffering and bereavement.

How amazing is the love of God! He will lovingly welcome, even in the hour of doubt.

> *And after eight days again his disciples were within, and Thomas with them: then came Jesus, the doors being shut, and stood in the midst, and said, Peace be unto you.*
>
> *Then saith he to Thomas, Reach hither thy finger, and behold my hands; and reach hither thy hand, and thrust it into my side: and be not faithless, but believing.*
>
> *And Thomas answered and said unto him, My Lord and my God.*
>
> *And Jesus saith unto him, Thomas, because thou hast seen me, thou hast believed: blessed are they that have not seen, and yet have believed.*
>
> JOHN 20:26-29

In the Hour of Failure

Failure is a bitter hour.

My father used to say, "We were all born to win. We know how to act then. But it takes awhile to learn to be a good loser." That was small comfort when I lost an elementary grade track meet, but I have remembered it often as an adult and gained from its wisdom.

We all strive for success. But anyone who achieves success has to walk through a flock of failures first. And it is in the hour of failure that some of our most valuable insights may be gained. For there is always something which can be learned from defeat. Every failure has some value for scrap. No battle is ever lost completely; something can always be salvaged.

Failure comes in all sizes and shapes and from many causes. Sometimes it comes through lack of skill or ability, sometimes by carelessness, sometimes by bad timing, sometimes by insufficient preparation, sometimes by injustice, sometimes by illness. But none is so small that it is inconsequential, and none is so large that it cannot be handled.

One of the most difficult lessons of life is to learn to accept the fact that there are inequalities, injustices, unpleasant facts which cannot be corrected. We have to begin with acceptance of some things and move from there. If we refuse to begin with that acceptance, we may hurl ourselves headlong into failure in the things that matter most in our lives.

One of my college students found the truth of this statement a few years ago. As a college senior the diagnosis of rheumatoid arthritis was given to her, and it shattered her world.

She cried; she raged; she screamed. She battered her mind against those words. But the fact remained immovable in the middle of her plans. At age twenty-one, she faced a lifetime with this disease as a companion.

And so Ann decided to show God that, if He could hurt her, she could lash back! And she did.

Her first step was to stop studying. Her 3.7 grade-point average plunged, and she took real satisfaction in the dismay of the professors who kept trying to figure out what was wrong.

Her next step was to quit dating the college boy who had been her steady for six months. She went to a drive-in one night determined to be a pickup. She was quickly successful and soon found herself in a parked car at the lake. Again she took real satisfaction in observing the frustration of her friends who could not understand what had happened to her innocent young life!

She stayed in school because she did not want to have an argument with her parents. She was bright enough to pull a C average without studying, and so her parents were not aware that anything was wrong.

A minister came to our college campus for a series of services. In one of the chapels, which Ann was required to attend, he talked about delayed gratification. He said that if we are at one point in life and we want to get to another, we have to pay the price to get there, regardless of how high that price might be.

He talked about professions. Ann knew that her real desire had always been to teach piano. She would be able to do this even when crippled. But she had chosen another course of study because she did not want to struggle with learning music theory. It was too late to change the degree program she was on, but she could go for another one afterward.

If she wanted to get from here to there, it would mean a price. But she could support herself even in a wheelchair.

Then the minister spoke of love. He said that if one wanted true, lasting love (which, of course, was her greatest desire), there was a price to be paid.

At that point, the tears came. Ann had already refused to pay the price. She could always come back to school for another degree, but she could never regain what she had lost in a parked car at the lake.

The rage, the hurt, the hopelessness engulfed her again. That night she refused to go to church. She went to the lake with a boy.

One day Ann came to see me. We had been very close friends before the advent of her illness. Since that time I had known she was avoiding me. But she had an "incomplete" in one of her classes, and she had to work it out before graduation. So she came.

We talked only about academics, and she turned to go. My heart went out to her, but I did not want to push. She paused at the door of my office, and then suddenly she whirled to sit in a chair and began to cry in great, heaving sobs.

I came and knelt in front of her and put my arms about her. I did not say anything. I just held her as she cried.

When the tears slowed, Ann said, "I've already told you about my problem."

"You told me about rheumatoid arthritis," I told her gently, "but that isn't your real problem."

Immediately her defenses were up. "Well—do tell me!"

"Your choice," I answered. "Your reaction."

"Choice?"

"You have a choice, you know. You can rebel, fight. You can stoically endure. Or—you can accept."

We talked for a long time about the road of accepting the fact of her disease and moving from there. It was a possibility she had not explored.

She promised to leave my office and go to the campus prayer chapel for meditation. Later, she told me that she had entered the small building and sat on the back pew. The sanctity of the atmosphere invaded her being. Ultimately she came to this resolution: Rheumatoid arthritis was not her choice. But God had allowed it to come into her life. She could accept that as a fact and go on from there, believing that He would walk with her even though her steps were painful and slow. If arthritis was to be her lot, she would learn to live with it.

She decided to graduate with her class and then begin preparation for a degree in music. She determined to pay the price of studying the hated theory to get from here, as a student, to there, as a piano teacher, her ultimate goal.

She resolved to drop her new "friends." She would never again go to the lake for a parking session. Perhaps, she prayed, the Lord, by His grace, would allow her the role of a loving, faithful wife.

Difficult? She found the days following her decision to be "hideously difficult." But she remained true in her resolve. Her B.A. complete, she is reaching even higher. Today, she is enrolled in a master's program in piano. And she is engaged to a shy, young lawyer.

The disease is still an unwelcome part of her life. But her daily prayer is that well-known one composed by Reinhold Niebuhr: "O God, give [me] serenity to accept what cannot be changed, courage to change what should be changed, and wisdom to distinguish the one from the other."

She had refused, at first, to accept an illness that could not be denied. That refusal hurled her headlong into failure. But in her hour of failure, she found God standing with her. And when she reached out for His loving strength and wisdom, she was able to walk from the hour of failure a wiser, more mature person and to fashion success and happiness from factors she had not chosen for herself.

The hour of failure is dark and painful for all of us. But we can take courage to reach again for fulfillment when we realize that we are not alone. Regardless of how big the problems we create in our lives—intentionally or unintentionally—we have a Redeemer God standing with us who will help us to make something satisfying and beautiful if we will allow Him. How amazing is the love of a God who will welcome us, even in the hour of failure.

> *The Lord is gracious and full of compassion; slow to anger, and of great mercy.*
>
> *The Lord upholdeth all that fall, and raiseth up all those that be bowed down.*
>
> *The Lord is nigh unto all them that call upon him, to all that call upon him in truth.*
>
> PSALM 145:8, 14, 18

In the Hour of Need

There was a young man in one of our churches who came to me and asked, "Is it OK to pray for things—you know—well, like help with college and stuff like that? They don't seem really related to religion, but they're important to me. Is it okay with God for me to ask Him to help me with the everyday problems of my world?"

What a thrilling answer I had to that question. If we give our hearts, souls, and minds to God, why should we not also give him our bodies with all their needs? This includes financial assistance in going to college, food and clothing for the body, knowledge for the mind—all the material necessities of our lives. He who notes the fall of the sparrow is interested in every area of our lives, and there is not a single aspect that falls outside His loving jurisdiction.

God gave us souls with which to worship. He gave us bodies in which our souls may dwell. In every aspect of our lives, He is with us, ready to help and assist—if we will let Him.

I first began to realize this when we were in our first pastorate, with a salary of twenty-five dollars per week. Economize and stretch as I would, there just *were* emergencies which arose that our available finances could not cover. And then fear would fill me; panic would take hold of my heart. "What will we do?" I moaned.

One morning I was telling the Lord about a certain large bill that had to be paid immediately, for which there were no funds available. Suddenly I felt a rebuke for my worry and panic. I paused in the midst of a sob, and my mind skipped back to college days when I had had no worries about material things. Why? Because my earthly father had given me a checkbook and promised that he would meet all my needs. All I had to do was write a check on his account, and the money would be mine. I looked at the Book in my hands and wondered why I could not have the same sense of serenity at this time, for had not my heavenly Father given me a "checkbook" of promises and assurances that He would care for me?

It was strange that this should be a new thought to me, but it was. My heavenly Father had promised in many places in the Bible to care for my needs just as my earthly father had promised to provide for my financial needs when I was in his care. I had not worried and wrung my hands in panic then; I had *trusted* the word of my earthly father. How much more, then, should I trust the Word of my heavenly Father!

Slowly I pondered this, letting the concept sink in. We were doing everything we could to handle our obligations as wisely as possible. This was all we could do. *He* had promised to do the rest. "Seek ye first the kingdom of God, and his righteousness; and *all these things* shall be added unto you" (Matthew 6:33). We were doing our part. Would it not be a *sin* not to trust Him to do His part?

Hesitantly at first, but gaining in courage, my prayer turned from one of doleful pleading to one of joyous praise and gratitude for the privilege of trusting His Word.

The next week from an unexpected source in an unexpected way, the exact amount for that bill was placed in our hands. But I possessed something of far greater value than a paid debt that day! I possessed a glowing and wonderful

truth: I need never allow panic, fear, or frustration to enter
my life again in regard to material necessities. I would do the
best I could with what I had. God would do the rest!

During these years of walking with Christ, I have kept a
little notebook in which I place a record of needs that have
arisen which were impossible for us to meet. Each of them,
without exception, has been met with just the amount needed
at just the right time—not always in the manner expected
but always adequate for our needs. Once it was in a sugar
bowl, with a note attached from a friend. Once it was in a
pile of diapers which were waiting to be folded. Once, on a
chicken's leg! God's emissaries of kindness adopted methods
that were sometimes startling and unusual! At any rate, when
we have done our best, we can rest assured that He will care
for our needs.

This was an exciting discovery to me. I had learned as a
child that we could give our hearts to God. In college I had
learned that we could give our minds to God. Now in this
small parish, I had learned that we could give our bodies to
Him—with all of their needs.

And how many times I have proved it!

I remember the day I took an aged dress from my closet
and buried my face in the shiny, outdated garment with its
yellowed collar, and cried. Years before, a generous lady had
given it to me from her lavish wardrobe. Now it eloquently
bespoke the many times of wear from both owners.

It was assembly time, and I hated the thought of once again
having to wear my "old faithful!" But I soon conquered my
impulse of grief and laid the blue dress on the bed ready for
pressing. Then I went back to the closet and took out the
hat. It was much too yellow to wear again this season without some work on it; so I went for the bottle of white shoe
polish which I used annually to perk up its color. (It is true:
Necessity *is* the mother of invention. The prospect of wear-

ing a shoe-polished hat may not be appealing to you, but just for fun, sometime, try it on an old hat. You'll be amazed!)

But as I worked over my garments, preparing them for the annual district assembly, there came a knock at the door. When I answered, a great box from a local department store was placed in my arms.

The deliveryman assured me he had the right address. Bewildered, I allowed him to leave and took the box into the bedroom. Wonderingly, I opened it. There, wrapped in tissue paper, was a fluffy, pink dress beset with bows in the most current fashion. Nestled next to it was a pink and white creation of net and flowers to thrill the heart of any hat wearer. I gazed at the contents of the box in awed delight.

And then I saw the note. It read: "I was young once and attended the annual assemblies with my preacher husband. I loved to have new things for the occasion. Won't you wear these with my love?"

It was unsigned.

I walked on wings of joy to that assembly session in my new, pretty clothes. Even though it was a minor need, God supplied.

My brother, Elton Wood, is a missionary to the Cape Verde Islands. In the summer of 1964, he and a national pastor from the islands, Jorge Barros, visited in our home.

After the evening meal I told them that I wanted to tell them a beautiful story. They were aware that the summer months of that year had been especially hard for us financially. My husband was attending the seminary in Kansas City, Missouri. He was going to school eight hours a day that summer, and most of our income depended upon my writing, which is erratic and insufficient for the full needs of a family. We had saved all we could to tide us over the summer, but it had been used up too soon. In August we were to the point where we would have to borrow money.

This return to graduate school had been a divinely ordered move in our lives. We knew we were in the will of God. We were striving to make ends meet, but we were nearing a financial crisis.

I had written eighteen booklets for a publisher that summer, and we were counting on that check to get us through the month. But it had not come. The first of the month came on Saturday. Our house payment was due. Eagerly I waited for the mail. Surely the check from the publisher would come! But there was none.

I knew there was no alternative. We would have to go to the bank on Monday and borrow money for the remaining weeks of the summer. Although we shrank from such a move, we felt it had to be done.

Sunday morning we drove out to our church in the country. The service progressed normally. At the close of his message, Bill asked the congregation to stand and prayed the prayer of dismissal. Then the chairman of the board walked to the front while everyone remained standing. He said a few words of appreciation for their pastor and handed Bill an envelope which contained, he said, "a token of love." Overcome with surprise, Bill thanked the people for their kindness. We both were thrilled with their thoughtfulness, and we knew that the probable twenty dollars or so contained in the envelope would be of great benefit at this time of financial strain.

We shook hands with our people, collected our Bibles and papers, and went to the car before we opened the envelope. When I opened it, over two hundred dollars fell out. It was enough to get us through the remaining weeks of summer!

Tears poured down my cheeks as I thanked God for the goodness and kindness of those wonderful people who were

willing to be *used* of God to help two of His children. We
had never mentioned our needs to them. The act was
prompted by love. We were overwhelmed with this reasser-
tion of the *fact* that God would be with us, even in our hour
of need.

When I finished telling this story, Jorge Barros began
speaking in Portugese and Elton interpreted for us. It was
another illustration of God's care in another land.

Jorge said that when he was a very small child in his
father's parsonage in the Cape Verde Islands, the usual finance
had not come in from the general church headquarters in
America for some time. The supplies of the family had
grown lower and lower until they had no food. Jorge's minister father rested in perfect faith and trust that all would be
cared for in the right time and in the right way. But one
morning, he sensed the distrust and fear of his child.

He took Jorge into a room away from the other members
of the family and closed the door. The two knelt to pray and
the father said, "Lord, I know that You will care for our
needs. But here is a little boy whose faith is being shaken because our money is gone and our food is gone. He has not
learned yet to understand that we, as Your children, shall
never want. Now I pray that You will send us finance just
now to strengthen the faith of this little boy."

Sitting in our living room, Jorge said with deep emotion,
"While we were still on our knees, there came a knock at
the door. When we opened the door, we found a cablegram
from America bearing the belated salary checks from the general church."

Whether in an American home, a Cape Verdian home, or
anywhere in all the world, the child of God can be serene.
For he has a heavenly Father who will care for us, even in the
hour of need.

And seek not ye what ye shall eat, or what ye shall drink, neither be ye of doubtful mind.

For all these things do the nations of the world seek after: and your Father knoweth that ye have need of these things.

But rather seek ye the kingdom of God; and all these things shall be added unto you.

LUKE 12:29-31

In the Hour of Old Age

This is the era when youth is coveted, sought after, worshipped. Those who are "full of years" seem always to be on the losing team.

The growing-up years, the adjustment years, the child-rearing years—all are a part of youth. The time of harvest comes in the despised period classified as old age.

Although this is general knowledge to most people, my mother never learned it. She never realized she was on the "losing team."

Mother was unconscious.

My father called with the report, and my husband and I drove all night to get to her. We raced into the hospital and saw my father talking with the doctor in the corridor. We joined them as the doctor was stating that Mother could never return home; she would have to have special care. He suggested a rest home.

I looked quickly at my father. Fiercely independent, he had cared alone for all of mother's needs. Although she was immobilized by illness, he had cooked her meals, washed her clothes, combed her hair. He did not want to let her go to a rest home.

But in the end, he agreed. And after a few trial weeks of unhappiness, he left their home to live with her in the rest home.

Mother responded to the treatment. In a few weeks, she

opened her eyes and demanded that the tubes be removed so she could get up. My father was overjoyed and immediately wanted to take her home.

But Mother knew that her illness had taken its last tenacious hold. She had fought it valiantly through the years; now it was winning. Although remaining in the rest home meant leaving a preciously loved world behind, Mother was certain of her decision.

She bent her efforts to making the rest home a beloved world. She made friends with the nurses and loved them as her own family. She made friends with the other residents and shared pictures of children and grandchildren. It seemed never to occur to her that it was not a blessed thing to be a senior citizen in a rest home.

Although she was in a wheelchair, she visited with the people up and down the halls. She attended the singing held each Tuesday night in the parlor, the church services held by the Christian church, the Christmas and Easter parties. She read books, played records, painted small ceramics, worked on scrapbooks for her grandsons, wrote letters, inspected flowers growing in the window, and rejoiced in the goodness of life.

Then blindness struck her. Still she tried to write me every week. The large letters ambled up and down the page and knocked into each other, but I could always make them relate her messages of love and cheer.

Soon even this was denied her. In her world of darkness, she listened to television; she had my father help her memorize Scripture; she played games of Bible quizzes and spelling challenges with anyone who was sport enough to be beaten. When she was alone, she told me, she would spell words backwards, quote poetry, and try to quote it backwards, also, just for fun. And she smiled. To everyone who came into the room, she gave a smile and her love.

My father read the Bible to her several hours each day. She spent a lot of time in prayer. And the dominant note of those prayers, as had been true through all of her life, was thanksgiving.

One of the last times I talked to Mother, I asked how she managed to be so radiant in the hour of old age. She did not hesitate for an answer.

"Oh honey, I had passed my allotted three-score years and ten before I came here. These are bonus years—bonus years with my husband, with my children. Because of that, they are *good* years."

"But you are bound to have periods of unhappiness at the loss of your home, your sight, your health—"

She nodded.

"Yes, there are pangs of unhappiness, but they are always *cushioned by gratitude:* gratitude for a husband whose love never fails; gratitude for children who are building useful, successful lives; gratitude for God, who has walked through all of life's changing seasons with me and who grows dearer each day! Even under less-than-ideal conditions I find life to be very *good* when cushioned by gratitude!"

Old age should be the "harvest years." But too often, it is easier to focus on the losses rather than the harvest. As I observed my mother in the hour of old age, I decided it was this thing called "focus" that made the difference.

Had she focused her energies and thoughts on the loss of her beloved home, her health, her sight, she could have been very miserable. But when she chose to focus on the "harvest," she was a beloved, beautiful person, a joy to everyone about her.

This importance of focus is as real in any hour of life as in the hour of old age. For it is true: our happiness and unhappiness depends, in great measure, on those things we *choose* to center our thoughts upon. Perhaps Paul said it best: "I have learned, in whatsoever state I am, therewith to be content" (Philippians 4:11*b*).

For parallelism, we could add: In whatsoever hour you find yourself, you may be content, for God has promised to work all things together for good, even in the hour of old age.

> *That the aged men be sober, grave, temperate, sound in faith, in charity, in patience.*
>
> *The aged women likewise, that they be in behaviour as becometh holiness, not false accusers, not given to much wine, teachers of good things;*
>
> *In all things showing thyself a pattern of good works.*
>
> TITUS 2:2-3, 7

In the Hour of Crisis

C. S. Lewis wrote in his *Letters to Malcolm:* "I certainly believe that to be God, is to enjoy an infinite present, where nothing has yet passed away and nothing is still to come." Viewed from our vantage point, this can give us insight into the sanity and the balance of God: He does not go to pieces in crisis times because He *is* in "an infinite present where nothing has yet passed away and nothing is still to come."

Not only does God not go to pieces in crises, He can keep us from going to pieces—if we will allow Him. He *knows* that whatever tragedy has hurled itself into our world, it has not *ruined* our world although He *knows* that it seems the end of our world to us. And because He is a Redeemer God, He will bring triumph even out of the hour of crisis—if we can open ourselves to Him.

I had always known this truth as good theory. But I never really tested it for myself until one October Sunday evening. My husband, Bill, was the substitute minister of a church in Duncan, Oklahoma.

He had preached in the morning service and was preparing for the evening service when he was stricken with pain. I was sitting in the congregation when he walked onto the platform. I knew immediately he was ill.

When the congregation stood for prayer, I saw him leave. With fear clutching my heart, I tiptoed out of the auditorium and made my way down the hallways to the pastor's study. By the time I opened the door, Bill lay unconscious on the floor.

I slipped back into the auditorium and asked a gentleman (whom I did not know) if he would take my husband to the hospital. He agreed and I went onto the platform and took Bill's chair. The service proceeded as usual.

The minister of music looked at me a bit oddly as he performed the various functions of the service. Finally, he stopped to whisper, "Are you going to speak?" I nodded. When the time came, he introduced me as the special speaker. He and the audience were totally mystified.

I stepped to the pulpit and made a brief explanation. Then I warned any young females in the audience considering marriage to a minister, "Whenever you marry a minister, you never know at what moment *you* may have to pray, speak, or die!"

There had been other times in our married life when, at a moment's notice, I had had to handle pulpit duties. But this was the most grave. Intuitively I knew that. But I also knew that Bill would have demanded that the service go on. An auditorium full of people come to worship needed a message. I attempted to fill the need.

When the service ended, I was taken to the hospital and informed that Bill had suffered a severe attack of diverticulitis. It would be a long, serious illness, I was told, and he should be transported immediately to the Oklahoma City hospital near our home.

I do not like to drive, and I did not have my driver's license with me. I had no idea how to get from Duncan to Oklahoma City. But they lifted Bill's unconscious form into the back seat of the car, and I started out.

I chattered away to the two children beside me in the front seat. I was desperately trying to keep their minds off the fear that lodged in all of our hearts.

I finally arrived in Oklahoma City but could not find the hospital. I drove around for many precious minutes desperately praying for the Lord to help me find that hospital. Later, friends asked why I did not stop and call for directions. It never once occurred to me. I had the responsibility and was trying my best to fulfill it.

Finally, the hospital emerged from the darkness. Attendants waited as I drove up; they had been alerted by the Duncan hospital. Bill was lifted out of the car and carefully taken into emergency and then into X-ray to see if the colon was perforated.

I parked the car and left my children in the corridor. I joined the doctors in X-ray as they were finishing. On the way back to emergency, I passed my children. Billy, my older son, was sitting stoically. Like his father, he never expressed emotion. But Ronnie, the youngest, was crying. I went to him and knelt beside him, cradling him in my arms.

He looked at me with all the agony of disillusionment in his eyes: "Mommy, God didn't answer my prayer! I prayed all the way here that God would make Daddy all better. And He didn't." Tears gushed. Head cuddled against my shoulder, he whispered, "Mommy, why didn't God make Daddy all better?"

I took a deep breath.

Oh boy! Theology right now! That's all I need.

At my promises to explain to him on the way home, he began to dry his eyes. I went on into the emergency room to find the doctor's verdict.

There would be no surgery that night. Treatment to prevent perforation had been started. We would wait.

Waiting, I discovered, was torturously difficult. The world stilled. The carousel stopped. There was no more sound of tinkling music, no more kaleidoscope of bright, dizzy colors. The world sat on its axis; the carousel poised on its platform—waiting tensely, waiting prayerfully, waiting lovingly, waiting.

And then on Friday, five days later, the colon did perforate. Emergency surgery was performed.

The surgeon was haggard when he gave me the report about *diverticuli, colostomy*—alien words that had no place in my world. When he was all finished, he sighed, "He is alive—for now."

When Bill was returned to his room, I took up my post of watching. And on envelopes, newspaper edges, any scrap of paper handy, my emotions poured forth in poetry. One midnight I wrote:

> "In sickness or in health—"
> I whispered the fine old words
> As a nineteen-year-old bride.
> I wore white lace;
> Candles flickered;
> His handclasp was strong.
>
> "In sickness or in health—"
> I did not know the meaning
> Of both words.
> Sickness was an alien word,
> Vague, ambiguous,
> Ill-defined.
> Only one thing
> I knew then,
> Besides health:
> Love.
> It was enough.
>
> "In sickness or in health—"
> I whisper the fine old words
> As a thirty-four-year-old wife.
> I wear red wool;
> A hospital light burns,
> His handclasp is weak.
>
> "In sickness or in health—"
> I know the meaning
> Of both words.

Sickness is a familiar word,
Common, close,
Clearly defined.
Only one thing
I know now,
Besides sickness:
Love.
It is enough.

It was Wednesday.

The doctor examined Bill. Then he called me into the hall. "He is on the edge," he said. "We are watching him carefully. He can go either way."

A few hours later I was called to the telephone at the nurse's station. I went to the phone and was informed that Ronnie, my younger son, had been hit by a car.

I hung up slowly.

Release! my brain screamed. *I cannot stand another fear!*

I turned and my head whirled. I thought I would faint.

And then—a verse of Scripture that I had memorized as a child flooded into my mind. The verse had never been especially meaningful—until now.

As I walked down the hospital corridor, I whispered the words to myself, "Thou wilt keep him in perfect peace whose mind is stayed on thee" (Isaiah 26:3).

"Thou wilt keep him in perfect peace, whose mind is stayed on thee."

And miraculously, by the time my hand touched the knob of Bill's door, that "perfect peace" was mine.

I had always wondered how I would react to crisis. I had been afraid that I would race up and down hospital hallways, pull my hair, shriek hysterically. But I discovered that in the hour of crisis our weakness is met with His perfect strength. I was able to walk through the hour of my deepest anxieties with serenity and perfect peace. It was uncharacteristic of me; it was characteristic of God.

Many days later, Bill opened his blue eyes to study me standing at the foot of his bed. Then in a natural voice he said clearly, "I love you." And I laughed and cried in the exhilaration of the moment. He would be all right.

Ronnie came through his crisis to enjoy all the attention he received from family and friends. And finally, we were all back together again as a family.

But only for a little while. Bill had another major operation, another attack of diverticulitis, a long period of convalescence. But the major crisis was passed. I had found a strength beyond my own. I *proved* His grace sufficient for my deepest needs.

And I felt an most overwhelming flood of gratitude for all that I had almost lost and for all that I had never really seen before. It was gratitude for the whole wonderful, terrible, unfathomable adventure of life and for all the little things, like the shout of a running little boy or a husband who cannot find his socks or a family seated at a table *together*. It was gratitude for all the big things, like birth and love and the fear of death, for this world and other worlds, for the flesh and for the spirit, for the moment and for eternity, for the miracle of prayer and the presence of God.

There can be perfect peace. Amazingly, incredibly, impossibly—there *can* be perfect peace, because there is never a moment when we stand alone. He has promised to be with us always, even in the hour of crisis.

> But now thus saith the Lord that created thee, O Jacob, and he that formed thee, O Israel, Fear not: for I have redeemed thee, I have called thee by thy name; thou art mine.
>
> When thou passeth through the water I will be with thee; and through the rivers, they shall not overflow thee: when thou walkest through the fire, thou shalt not be burned; neither shall the flame kindle upon thee.
>
> For I am the Lord thy God, the Holy One of Israel, thy Saviour.   ISAIAH 43:1-3

In the Hour of Death

Death is universal. The ultimate statistic, as G. B. Shaw once said, is the same: "One out of one dies." Death is every man's problem.

There is a lot of death-talk in modern conversation. Jean-Paul Sartre says death is absurd, something that renders life irrational. Therefore, he says, we ought not to think about it. Martin Heidegger comes to the opposite conclusion: Death is an essential strand in the fabric of life. "To think about death," he says, "is part of living." Disdaining talk, the Christian *sings* about death, not as one "singing in the rain," but as one who, though he must die, knows of the death of death! Death is not a fearsome, awesome finality; death is merely a transition, a door into a larger life. This was asserted and proven by the God-man, Jesus Christ.

There are many views and philosophies about the hour of death. My mother chose the Christian view.

Because I was her youngest child (a totally unexpected "blessing" after nine years of having her family completed), I was only fifteen when she was stricken with Parkinson's disease. The illness pushed her through progressive stages of slow, painful walking to a wheelchair to blindness to bed-fastness to thirteen months of unconsciousness to death. Because I was the only child in the house (my youngest brother went to college when I was eight), Mother and I had an intensely close, warm relationship.

71

I stood by her bed in the early hours of that February morning as my mother's body drew the last breaths of life. *Mother!* my heart cried, *don't go, not without a word! Mother! You must say something!* We, who had shared our every thought, our every philosophy, surely could not be parted without a word. *Say something, Mother,* I silently pleaded.

Then, suddenly, I knew that words in the hour of death were not necessary for us. Everything important had already been said. I watched her body grow still without a word, and I knew it was all right.

Throughout her life she had tried to articulate her feelings. Even her concern for my reaction to this moment was shown in one of her last letters to me. Then almost blind, Mother had written, in scrawling letters which rambled up and down the page, this note:

> Ruth dear, I have been thinking of how close we have been through the years of your life. You came to me a gift from the hand of God, and I have rejoiced in that gift ever since. We have experienced joy and sorrow, tragedy and triumph together. But now as I approach the time of my going home, I want to tell you something that you must remember when you are bidding my body good-bye. Ruth, my child, do not ever say, "Mother is dead." Just know that I'm away—I've gone on ahead to a better land—and one day you'll come, and we'll again join hands.
>
> Ruth, don't think of my sadness at leaving this world where I have known so much joy. But instead, dear little girl, think
>
> Of your mother stepping on shore and finding it heaven
> Of her taking hold of a hand and finding it God's hand
> Of her breathing a new air and finding it celestial air
> Of her feeling invigorated and finding it immortality
> Of her stepping from storm and darkness and tempest to an unknown calm
> Think, Ruth, of your mother waking up and finding it home.

This was her faith. That early February morning, I stood by her bed as her faith became her *fact!*

After a few moments, I went to call my husband and my brothers. Then we gathered about Daddy's bed where he lay sleeping. He had never left Mother during the long years of her illness. He had been by her side every moment during the long months of her unconsciousness. Gently my brother Joe awakened him.

I took a deep breath; the moment I had dreaded had come. How would Daddy react?

"What's wrong?" Daddy asked.

"Mother went to heaven a few minutes ago," Joe said.

As the tears began down Daddy's cheeks, he said with a wistful smile, "She's happy."

I looked over at mother's still body lying on the other bed, and I knew he was right. Somewhere she *was* happy.

Joe said, "Daddy, if what you have preached all these years is true, Mother is running for the first time in years, singing for the first time in months, laughing and free!" And we, who loved her, held hands for strength and rejoiced in her release.

When the men came with the stretcher, they tenderly lifted the fragile shell from the bed. They seemed to know that the spirit which had dwelt there had been special. I followed as they rolled the covered form down the hall to the waiting ambulance. I watched as they lifted it into the back and closed the doors, and then they climbed into the front. As they started the vehicle, moving it slowly away with its precious burden, I whispered, "O God, I thank You so much that I *know* they are not taking away my mother!"

Later, I wrote:

My mother's body
lies in a
pink-lined casket.
Her familiar
hands
are folded;

her always-smiling
face
is serene.
People come and say
good-bye
as if they believe
she is dead.
By their tears
of finality
I can see
that they have missed
the whole point
of death.

My mother was full of
bright life,
easy laughter,
quick forgivingness,
indomitable courage,
quicksilver delight.
And when her
body wore out,
she went away.
Don't you see?
This is not she.

This was the house
in which she lived.
This was her set of tools
with which she worked.
I love this frail shell
lying in the
pink-lined casket;
I love it because she once lived there,
because she once used her
hands
eyes
mouth
feet
to care for me

and give me love.
But this is not she.

She is far away,
But all about us, still
Savoring the new
adventure—
Life eternal:
Laughing,
Caring,
Relishing
In a dimension
We cannot conceive of.

Weep tears of sorrow
for our temporary loss,
but do not weep
tears of finality,
for we shall see her
again.
Weep tears of pain
at our separation,
but do not weep
tears for my mother:
This is her
Coronation Day!

At her graveside, my oldest brother stood and read aloud my mother's letter to me in which was expressed her faith about the hour of death. And we, who listened, felt a surging rush of triumph. Mother's faith was now her fact—"Because Death is only a door into the larger life."

And even through our tears, we smiled in the hour of death. Jesus Christ had walked out of a rock-sealed tomb and conquered death. We knew there was nothing to fear.

Our mother had simply stepped onto another shore—and found it heaven. She had taken hold of a hand—and found it God's hand. She had felt invigorated—and found it immortality.

How amazing is the love of a God who welcomes us, even in the hour of death.

> *And I heard a voice from heaven saying unto me, Write, Blessed are the dead which die in the Lord from henceforth: Yea, saith the Spirit, that they may rest from their labours; and their works do follow them.*
>
> Revelation 14:13

In the Hour of Sorrow

In the hour of death, God gives to His children extra measures of grace. We are made conscious of His presence in new and marvelous ways. His love seems to literally *lift* the spirit's focus to the promises and hope of immortality. I think Mother's hour of death was in many ways the most extraordinary experience of God's presence I have ever had. It was glorious and wonderful beyond belief.

But this heightened understanding and joy of immortality does not last forever. We, who are of the earth, have to come back to earth. And we have to live on it with the loss of one deeply beloved. This task is neither glorious nor wonderful; it is excruciatingly painful.

I began to discover this immediately upon my return home.

When I was called to Mother's bedside, I had been working on the production of several television programs. I had left the manuscripts and instructions concerning how they could be produced at the scheduled time. When I came home, I found that the programs were still waiting for me. Production had been postponed until my return.

Somehow sensing the approaching dissolution of my victory over Mother's death, I walked slowly into the television studio. I greeted the performers and picked up the folder containing the scripts and opened it. The first program format began with a poem written by my mother, "Oh! I sing with the joy of life!"

But she was dead, gone forever from my world. She would never write another poem. I would never again hear her sing with the joy of life.

And in that moment the triumphant calm began to shatter into little pieces. Intellectually I understood the joy and certainty of immortality. Emotionally I began to understand how different life would be without my mother.

It made no difference that she had lain in unconsciousness for thirteen months prior to her death. I had always believed she would surely open her eyes one morning and say, "Oh! I sing with the joy of life!" She had never been lost to me— until that moment.

Suddenly I wanted to hold up the scripts and shout at the people waiting for my directions, "My mother's dead! My mother's dead!"

Silently, I cried, *O God, why did my mother have to die? Why my mother? Why mine?*

There were no answers in the eyes of the waiting performers. I knew the answers would be long in coming. I took a deep breath. "Margo to the park setting; Camera one." It was going to be a long, difficult night.

Somehow the days moved by. Friends tried to reach out but there was nothing to say. They were helpless in the face of death, just as I was. There were no words. We all have to die, but we cannot talk about it. Tragedy is our heritage, and yet we cannot cope with it.

Mine was not the only mother to die, but it was a unique event. Neither friends nor relatives could talk to me about it. "I don't know what to say," they would falter. But their caring enough to hold out their hands was meaningful; I was grateful that they tried.

And how much more helpful were those who silently, falteringly, held out their hands to me than those who tried to dispense wisdom in pat clichés, those who surely had never walked in the hour of sorrow. Clichés had no place; this was stark reality.

"You'll soon forget," blithely chirped one woman.

I inwardly writhed at the thought.

My mother was radiant, beautiful, vibrant. I did not want to *forget*. She was a part of me. Although the earthly presence had been stripped away, the *essence* of that indomitable spirit remained in memory.

"Do you remember that summer her illness began?" I would ask my brother. "Do you remember how she memorized chapters of the Bible to keep her mind off the pain? Do you remember— Do you remember—"

With my mind on a million other demands, I would suddenly laugh. Her laugh. The sound brought back the dreadful pain. I was probably more like her than anyone else. And the way I laughed, the way I phrased a sentence, the way I cocked my head as I looked into the mirror to comb my hair reminded me of her. Forget? Oh no!

The powerful explosion of grief may pass, but my memories will be with me always.

"It all has been God's will," comforted a minister who should have known better.

My anger rose.

God's will that my mother be stricken by disease?

God's will that she be crippled for years?

God's will that she lose her sight and voice?

God's will that she lie unconscious for thirteen months?

God's will that she die in a sore-infested body?

God, whose name is love,

    whose nature is compassion,

    whose Spirit is goodness,

willed all this?

God *permitted* all this to happen: disease, incapacitation, death. But I cannot believe that God *willed* these years of her pain. Such willing would not be consistent with His nature.

My mother died. I do not know why God *permitted* her to die that way. I do not know why this loss to our family had to occur at this time. But I am persuaded that "all things (the things we understand and those we do not; the triumphant and the tragic) work together for good to them that love God, to them who are the called according to his purpose" (Romans 8:28).

Could I believe that God, who had enabled my mother to live a life that was so attractive to her children that they adored her, who had enabled her to smile through the years in spite of a steadily encroaching disease, who had enabled her to write of approaching death with such faith—could I believe that that God would desert Mother in death and me in life? No. Even in the midst of pain, I knew I could not.

I had no idea how God would work all things together for good in the hour of sorrow, but I could sense Him steadily asking me to believe that He would. Such working might be intensely painful, but it would make me free. God would work all things together to give greater strength, deeper wisdom, wider understanding in the midst of sorrow.

O Lord, I began to pray, *may I in the darkness of this hour draw closer to You than is possible in the sunshine. Only then—only then may Thy will be done!*

Through the hour of death, where His grace may lift one to new heights, and through the hour of sorrow, where His strength may enable one to walk through new depths, His loving presence abides. God is love, even in the hour of sorrow.

> *In the day when I cried thou answeredst me, and strengthenedst me with strength in my soul.*
> *The Lord will perfect that which concerneth me: thy mercy, O Lord, endureth for ever.*
>   PSALM 138:3, 8

In the Hour of Bitterness

A promise is a covenant between two people to do or not do a specific thing. The Bible is filled with promises that God makes to man.

"The LORD is my rock, and my fortress, and my deliverer; my God, my strength, in whom I will trust; my buckler, and the horn of my salvation, and my high tower. I will call upon the LORD, who is worthy to be praised: so shall I be saved from mine enemies" (Psalm 18:2-3).

Happiness can come to our lives when we understand these promises clearly. Bitterness can enter our world when we misunderstand, when we believe the promises will protect our lives from unpleasantness.

One of my college students had memorized these promises since childhood. He believed that they were covenants that God would protect him and his loved ones from all who would hurt and damage. When he discovered his error, he became the victim of bitterness. Let him tell his story.

* * *

My world caved in the night of my high school baccalaureate.

My father is a minister. He preached the sermon for the service, which was held in our church. I was thrilled, proud, determined to follow my father's call to go forth to serve. My heart was a flaming altar for a just, good God.

81

The service ended. I walked back to the platform after the recessional to talk with my father, whom I admire as a saint of God. A church board member joined us.

Ignoring my presence, he said, "You are nothing but a hypocritical bag of wind! To call you a minister is to defy everything holy. I will do all in my power to see you ousted from the pulpit forever."

It was the inexcusable outcry of one man against a man ordained of God. I was certain that God would lift up His arm to destroy this miserable creature and that His wrath would come down upon him with the speed of lightning.

But nothing happened.

In the paralyzing silence that followed, the God of my childhood seemed to gather Himself up sadly from the dirt into which He had been thrown and limp away—beaten.

My father put his hand on my shoulder. "We will pray about this," he said.

And we prayed, oh, how we prayed through the weeks that followed. We prayed with pain and sorrow, but God did not answer.

There were wild accusations made, long emotional meetings. I hated these people who were tearing at my father the way a dog tears at a piece of meat. My anger grew until it splashed over to encompass God. Where was He? Why did He not make His presence known? Or was He indifferent to our needs—a lofty God in isolation who did not care for His children?

And since there was no answer, my heart left its love for God, and I walked alone.

But my father continued his loving ministry to the people. I watched him carefully and decided that he was like Job, singing praises to the Lord unendingly, no matter what. I did not have Job's faith, but he, like Job, prayed with tender obedience. I did not pray at all.

Fall came, and he wanted me to go to college. Because I did not want to hurt him, I went. But I was lonely. I had given up the love that had embraced me, and college was no substitute.

Just before Christmastime, things came to a final crisis in the church, and my father resigned. I was frozen with bitterness and hatred toward those who could not love this wise, gentle man who talked to them of God. My bitterness and hatred encompassed God himself, who seemed to have stood by unmoved. He had promised, but He had done nothing. He had all power, but He stood idly by and let evil run rampant. Suddenly I imagined my father beside the myriad of other Christian martyrs—and I saw God laughing!

A true God could not be evil. If all this could happen and go unpunished, there simply was no God. The verses I had memorized from the Bible were not promises at all! And with this new, bitter atheism, terror seized me; and something within me withered. I walked about the campus, living yet dead inside. And nobody seemed to notice.

My father went to pastor another church. He continued to pour out love upon those of his parish. I watched him in wonderment. How could he possess so much love? I knew he still prayed for the members of his former parish. His love came from God, he said.

I do not really know how I allowed myself to go inside the college prayer chapel one spring afternoon; I had never been inside. But I did go inside and sat on the back pew.

A red-haired girl was kneeling at the altar in front. She was crying. Unashamedly I listened to her prayer. It went something like this:

"Give me strength, O Lord, to accept my place in Your world. I am not Your only child. May I not rebel against the sorrow, pain, and burdens that come into my life as You work with Your other children."

I leaned forward and put my head on the seat in front of me. Could this be my answer? God had not failed me, hidden himself from me. He was not my private God. I had no special rights. He would not cut off some men because they erred against me. He lovingly worked in all of us to free us from selfishness, greed, and self-importance. He love those who hated my father, just as He loved my father and me. His love encompassed us all.

Right there I opened my heart to God once more and asked for His forgiving grace. Suddenly there was peace within. And I wept, not from bitterness as before but because the ring of steel around my heart was broken. I was finally free from hatred and doubt. And John Wade's hymn sang in my heart:

> "The flame shall not hurt thee;
> I only design
> Thy dross to consume,
> And thy gold to refine."

The world was dipped in sunshine when I walked out of the prayer chapel. I stood and looked about the college campus and whispered *promises* I had learned long ago:

"He healeth the broken in heart, and bindeth up their wounds. He telleth the number of the stars; he calleth them all by their names (Psalm 147:3-4). Great is our LORD, and of great power: his understanding is infinite. . . . Peace I give unto you" (John 14:27).

Healing had begun within me.

*   *   *

We can come to know God in Jesus Christ. When we know Christ well enough, we know that He not only *gives* peace; He *is* our peace! We can remember the promises of God as we look at the complexities of our world. We can know Him to be a God of His Word when we come to understand Him in Jesus Christ. Here lies the clarification: "No man hath seen God at any time; the only begotten Son, which is in the bosom of the Father, he hath declared him" (John 1:18). Jesus Christ can show us the heart of God and dissolve negative feelings into deep, quiet peace.

Jesus Christ can do this for us, even in the hour of bitterness.

Let all bitterness, and wrath, and anger, and clamour, and evil speaking, be put away from you, with all malice:
And be ye kind one to another, tenderhearted, forgiving one another, even as God for Christ's sake hath forgiven you.

EPHESIANS 4:31-32

In the Hour of Helplessness

One day when I was a student at the University of Kansas, I was in a doctor's office to be treated for a cold. An emergency arose, and he had to excuse himself.

When he returned, he said, "One of the most prevalent illnesses we treat on this campus is attempted suicide. Students get caught up in the grip of circumstances they feel helpless to change, and they find no way out of their predicament except the way of self-destruction."

I have thought about his words often. Helplessness is terrifying. We struggle against it; and yet is it not true that in the hour of helplessness, we might find the greatest glory of God's grace? The psalmist wrote, "I was brought low, and he helped me" (116:6). I have slowly begun to believe that it is this hemming-in process, this stripping of all our self-sufficiencies, this bringing us face to face with our personal helplessness that teaches us most clearly that God is gloriously adequate for all of our problems.

This truth was brought home to me in our first parish. It happened our first Christmas there. The youth activity we chose for the holiday season was the presentation of a living tableau of the manger scene, held in front of the church each night of the week prior to Christmas.

For days leading up to Christmas week, we had been in a dither of activity making costumes, erecting a stable, acquiring animals, working with the cast. One afternoon I drove to the church with a large sack filled with costume materials. I dropped it on the front pew and pulled out a long piece of burlap. I appraised its suitability for a costume and then draped it about me to see how it would look.

A voice broke the stillness of the empty church. "You look much prettier without the burlap!"

I wheeled about and beheld a dark-haired, neatly dressed man of middle age approaching from the rear pews. His dark eyes were merry with the pleasure of having thus surprised me.

"I—why—hello!" I said, trying to be gracious.

"Sorry to startle you," he said. "I'm visiting in town for a few days, and I've been interested in the beehive of activity over here. Working on a manger scene, I take it?"

"That's right," I answered, pleased with his interest. "Our church teens are doing it. We'd like you to come by and see it some night."

"Now would you?" he asked softly with a bemused smile. Then he added, "I wonder about that, because, you see, I don't believe in your scene. I'm an atheist."

The piece of burlap slipped from my hands. My face must have worn the naked look of surprise.

"Does that surprise you?" he asked. "Don't you know that there are plenty of people who don't swallow this Christmas stuff?" He looked at me appraisingly. "You're an intelligent young woman. I've observed you. And yet, you believe it, don't you?"

"With all my heart!"

"I can understand these kids believing it; they don't know any better. But you're educated. You should know better."

"I know that the Christmas story is true!"

"Don't say you 'know.' Say you 'believe.' "

"I know!" I said firmly. "I know in my heart."

"You believe in something that you can't prove."

Aghast, I answered, "But I can prove it. I can prove it by the Bible."

He laughed. "Now really! The Bible was written by men. Men make mistakes and errors and dream impossible dreams." He shook his head. My mind turned desperately back through college classes, church youth groups, Sunday school lessons for an answer to give him. I found one.

"Error dies; truth lives," I replied with a note of triumph. "The Bible has not only lived but has increased in influence through the years."

"But you must admit that the majority of the peoples of the world are not followers of Christianity." And he proceeded to give me some facts and figures he remembered. I listened intently, all the time searching his face, seeking an answer.

"I believe there was a man named Jesus who lived in Palestine," he said. "I can't believe he was divine."

How I longed for my theologically trained husband to be present. But this was my battle. I knew that I could not tear down his learned arguments; so it was a few moments before I spoke.

"I can't debate the point with you," I said, "for I am not that wise. But your arguments aren't the real issue anyway. The things of the Spirit can't be reduced to neat formulas. They have to be understood through faith."

He snorted.

"The spiritual world may be intangible," I added, "but it is fact."

He looked at me keenly. "The only things that are fact in this world are the things we can touch and see and smell. We have to fight with our own strength and no one else's!" Then he laughed. "You're pretty intense about all of this. Do you still want me to come to your manger scene?"

I nodded slowly. "Very much."

"Why?"

"It could do you good."

He looked at me strangely. "You really think I'm wrong, don't you?"

I nodded. "Don't you?"

He grinned. "I concede the possibility, but not the probability."

The silence was tense between us. This was my first challenge as a minister's wife, and I could not meet it.

Just then a car door slammed in front, and the happy laughter and noise of teenage voices came to us. He turned to go.

"Will you promise me something?" I asked impulsively. "Would you promise—well, if somehow you come to know that there is strength beyond the human—would you come?"

He smiled. "Of course."

He walked out of the door past the young people as they swarmed into the church. My hands were soon busy with shepherds' robes and angel wings.

Each night of Christmas week I searched for that man's face in the crowd that gathered to view the manger scene and in the cars which slowed on the highway, but he was never there.

Then it was Christmas Eve.

The tableau spotlighted on the church lawn was at its best. The girl portraying Mary looked as I thought that other Mary must have looked so long ago. The others standing about her completed our reproduction of the most beautiful picture in the world!

Again I searched the faces of those who came or drove past, but the one I looked for did not appear. It was a chill night, and I thought I would step inside the church for a few minutes.

I made my way to the front door, and as I started to open

it, a figure came around the side of the church.

It was the stranger.

He stood there not saying anything; and when he finally spoke, his voice was husky. I strained my ears to hear.

"Today," he said, "I was staying at a friend's home on the bayou while they went shopping. Their little girl fell into the water. She went under." He knotted his hands together. "I was scared. I can't swim, but I knew I had to get to her. I jumped in; and I don't know how, but I finally got her out of the water. There was a car there, but I don't know how to drive. But I was desperate, so I lifted her in and started the motor. By some miracle I got it moving. When we reached the main road, I hailed someone who took us the rest of the way to a hospital. She'll be all right."

His face was drawn as he said, "I told you that if I came to know strength beyond the human, I would come."

He turned slowly and walked toward the manger scene brightly lit against the Christmas Eve sky.

I watched him standing there, looking at the scene, and it seemed that his figure was a symbol of man toiling and striving through all of life's varied hours—until he is confronted with the grace of God in Jesus Christ. Reaching the end of himself and looking up at last to the source of hope and power, he had found strength beyond his own.

That strength is available to us all if we will only accept it. We may find His sufficiency. "My strength is made perfect in weakness," He said. That strength is ours for the taking, even in the hour of helplessness.

> *I will lift up mine eyes unto the hills; from whence cometh my help.*
>
> *My help cometh from the Lord, which made heaven and earth.*
>
> *The Lord shall preserve thy going out and thy coming in from this time forth, and even for evermore.*
>
> PSALM 121:1-2, 8

Epilogue

The Lord God omnipotent reigneth!

It was this firm conviction that God was in control of the world, the universe, and their personal lives that gave the three Hebrew children the indomitable courage to stand befor the king, in their hour of decision, and boldly declare their total allegiance to divine authority.

Animated by this same confidence, Martin Luther, in his hour of challenge, stood before Charles V and resolutely declared that he was a prisoner of the Word of God and could pursue no other course than to follow its teachings.

And myriad heroes of the cross today are confronting equally insurmountable tasks with the same kind of faith and courage. These heroes believe that God's grace is sufficient for the need of *any* hour.

They do not believe that walking with God is a guarantee against problems; they believe that walking with God is a guarantee against *defeat!* He never promised that if we followed His leading, we would never know frustration, weakness, or pain. Instead He promised something infinitely more precious. He told us that when we are in our hours of frustration, weakness, and pain, *He will be there with us.*

Through His Word He tells us, "I know you—as you are! I know the reason behind each failure and each success of your life. I know the consequences of each of those events. You do not have to explain yourself to Me. I already know all

93

about you. I know all that is good. I know all that is bad. I am by your side when you laugh with joy and hold life closely to your heart. I am with you when you suffer heartbreak. I stand with loving arms outstretched to welcome you into my love, *even when you cry.*"